AF270294

NIGHT
OWL

ALSO BY AIMEE NEZHUKUMATATHIL

Bite by Bite: Nourishments and Jamborees (essays)

Lace & Pyrite: Letters from Two Gardens (a chapbook with Ross Gay)

*World of Wonders: In Praise of Fireflies, Whale Sharks,
and Other Astonishments* (essays)

Oceanic (poems)

Lucky Fish (poems)

At the Drive-In Volcano (poems)

Miracle Fruit (poems)

NIGHT

POEMS

OWL

AIMEE NEZHUKUMATATHIL

Am imprint of HarperCollins*Publishers*

Without limiting the exclusive rights of any author, contributor or the publisher of this publication, any unauthorized use of this publication to train generative artificial intelligence (AI) technologies is expressly prohibited. HarperCollins also exercise their rights under Article 4(3) of the Digital Single Market Directive 2019/790 and expressly reserve this publication from the text and data mining exception.

NIGHT OWL. Copyright © 2026 by Aimee Nezhukumatathil. All rights reserved. No part of this book may be used or reproduced in any manner whatsoever without written permission except in the case of brief quotations embodied in critical articles and reviews. For information, address HarperCollins Publishers, 195 Broadway, New York, NY 10007. In Europe, HarperCollins Publishers, Macken House, 39/40 Mayor Street Upper, Dublin 1, D01 C9W8, Ireland.

HarperCollins books may be purchased for educational, business, or sales promotional use. For information, please email the Special Markets Department at SPsales@harpercollins.com.

Ecco® and HarperCollins® are trademarks of HarperCollins Publishers.

hc.com

FIRST EDITION

Designed by Alison Bloomer
Owl illustration © Mateusz/stock.adobe.com

Library of Congress Cataloging-in-Publication Data

Names: Nezhukumatathil, Aimee author
Title: Night owl : poems / Aimee Nezhukumatathil.
Description: First edition. | New York, NY : Ecco, 2026.
Identifiers: LCCN 2025029669 (print) | LCCN 2025029670 (ebook) | ISBN 9780063282315 hardcover | ISBN 9780063282322 trade paperback | ISBN 9780063282339 ebook
Subjects: LCGFT: Poetry
Classification: LCC PS3564.E995 N54 2026 (print) | LCC PS3564.E995 (ebook)
LC record available at https://lccn.loc.gov/2025029669
LC ebook record available at https://lccn.loc.gov/2025029670

Printed in the United States of America

26 27 28 29 30 LBC 5 4 3 2 1

for my owlets

What hath night to do with sleep?

—JOHN MILTON

CONTENTS

midnight ✦✦°✦

the darkest hour is just before dawn ✦⁺˚✦

crepuscule

NOCTURNE FOR DARK THINGS

I do my finest listening in the dark.
My best friend has always been ink
and she lets me talk so much at night.

One of the marvels of my life—
an alphabet. A whole green and mossy
world can be made and remade

from just twenty-six dark curlicues.
Here's more dark: sometimes birds sleep
tucked under a giraffe's dusky armpit

and sometimes fungi fatten only at night.
When I was a kid, I used to worry over
so many bugs and moths slamming

into our windshield. My sons have never
known that concern, which is another kind
of worry. But dark marvels still bloom

and snick the soil, swim the oceans and air—
and even on the moon: wide, flat plains
are called seas, lakes, and marshes. Bays

are named Joy, named Sorrow, named Hope,
named Nectar, named Softness, named Serpent,
named Stickiness, named Tranquility, named

Clouds, named Sleep, and my favorite—named Love.

SOLAR ECLIPSE

Hot Springs National Park

Four-year-olds ask about 250 questions a day
so by the time they are five, they will have asked
about 180,000 questions. Most of us stop asking
anything at all in middle school. Most of us
don't need to be told not to look at the sun during
an eclipse. But the geese at the lake nip the moss
like it's green shortbread, and evidence of love
is all around us. In Tagalog, *mahal kita* means
I love you, and for 3 minutes and 38 seconds, the moon
loved the sun. When we argue about stars and who sees
them, and who or what cannot—we get clouds stretched
over all our eyes. How do we capture the magic
of strangers resting in a park full of blankets and chairs
with the gurgle of warm and bubbly water rippling
all around us for our otherwise quiet soundtrack? How
do we say mahal kita to strangers? How do we stay
curious as we swim in this life, kicky paddle feet hurrying
towards a new thing? Silly goose, just say it: mahal kita!
After it's over, why do some of us forget to look up
and notice the rise, the sparkle, what still glows in the sky?

HOW TO BUILD A MOON GARDEN WHEN THE NEWS IS ALL HORROR

To see where the moon melts over the garden,
or where the bats flit, or where the air sweetens

    with pollen and moth-frenzy, I recommend
    a night walk to discern the perfect patch for it.

Under this glow, we could all use a distraction—
dig with a silver shovel and choose colors that swoon

    and moan under our satellite: dusty pinks,
    baby blue, lavender, white, and butter yellow gems

unfurl at dusk until dawn. Sometimes moonflower
vining over a trellis looks like a waterfall

    out of the corner of your eye. So many to choose from:
    evening primrose, night-blooming jasmine, heliotrope,

tuberose, four o'clocks, lamb's ears, astilbe, calla lily, white clematis,
fairy candles, periwinkles, and you can even launch snowballs

    in summer with creamy oak hydrangeas. Turn off the hiss
    and whir from man-made lights and walk the night,

walk the grass, the fence line, let your boot crackle over
pebble and stick bits. Careful if skunks shuffle over to see what

all the fuss is about. Don't tussle with weeds. If you set
your shovel down, skunks won't bother you at all.

And on the off chance they do, at least the spray might
sizzle like stars. Bats swoop and fly erratic, but birds

glide between wing flap—that's how you can tell what
flutters across a lake moon. If you make a moon garden,

even the dark lapping of water under a duck-shush of wave
won't be louder than the silver in your own bright yard.

PUNCTUATION

WHAT I LEARNED
IN GREENLAND

Ilulissat

I thought I understood summer for example—
the season of fruit and firefly glow—but I never
knew it with the midnight sun on my face. Now
I know summer as polka dots of sunburst lichen—

like ellipses across big folds of gneiss and granite
hills. And summer now will always mean *ice*
to me, because if the ice sheet were to melt
and flow into the ocean, the sea level would rise

over twenty feet. And the Earth would spin
more slowly—the length of the halibut day
growing longer by about two milliseconds.
And though I always want more time with you,

I'll gladly give those up so I can remember
summer from the flip and hook-twist of a spotted
wolf fish gnashing at the line. I hope summers always
pop and crack like doors slammed in a hurry

from icebergs' breath, and stretch the horizon
wide in pink sunlight. There are not enough words
in the Kalaallisut language (or any language)
to prepare you for the five hundred shades of blue

in icebergs. No matter how many Mississippi summers
I drink up, even in July—I know at least three fin whales
who promised me clap-slap and sea spray if I return—
a particular round of icy applause I'll never forget.

LETTER FOR NOCTILUCA

(proper name for sea sparkle or sea fire)

It's been so long since I heard from you
when I finally did, I was like a sandpiper
hearing thunder for the first time. You used to visit
my shore often, lap my ankles with your foamy laugh.
When I see your name, my heart claps like clamshell
or coquina—or a scallop tambourine with dark stars
of shark teeth along the wrack. Even just hearing
your laugh sends me into a fig-sugar crumble. I hear
reports of lit-up mangroves, full of reptiles
that don't know what to call the flecks of light on their backs.
You kiss me on the cheek in full view of others. We hold
each other a beat too long. We pledge ourselves to snow
to pink sand to fresh redbud shoots iced overnight
when nothing moves except winter stars—

    like Procyon   like Betelgeuse   like Sirius, the dog star.

FIREFLY ARS POETICA

It's no secret I'm a summer gal. I adore the bevy & bounty of stone
fruit & sun-drenched gardens, pool-plashes from my teen sons, &
so much green & bloom & chirp in the thick canopy of trees arched
above me. When we enter a season of shorter days & winter, I too
want to overwinter like bumble bees, brown bears, & wood frogs.
I look to my favorite summer creature—the firefly—to help guide
the way. I prefer small lamps. I prefer no music, save the times I
can hear my own heart slam underneath my blouse. I prefer writing
everything by pencil: the *shhh-shhh-shhh* of the lead on the page &
the satisfying scritch of crossing out feels like I'm making
something. Clicks of the keyboard sound like high heels walking
nowhere in particular. Sometimes I revise. Sometimes I stick
on a word & cannot move on—like my shield or scutellum
(the hard, triangle-shaped covering on a firefly's body where
the wings begin) makes me feel shy, protective. Sometimes I dial up
the music & sound play. I revise. When the music of a sentence seems
to be nonexistent, I worry. I revise again. One thing to remember:
sometimes you are in a quiet season. Sometimes you can hear
the patter of a leaf (or three) muttering at your feet. Maybe you read
or scoop & sieve books for later. Fireflies spend most of their brief life
as larvae after all, covered under leaf litter, gathering up food during
the winter to gain strength. Do not worry if this is not your season.
It will come. I am certain of it. It will come. In the world of fireflies,
that quiet is called the larval stage. And one of the gabillion kajillion
magical things about fireflies? Don't forget—even their larvae *glow*.

ARCHES NATIONAL PARK
SUNSET HAIBUN

The last time Polaris looked this way and was surrounded by all its friends in the
mountains means this park will bend light if we face west. Nothing prepares you for the size
of the arch the wild bend and blow this arch of stone hundreds of thousands of years around the

time *Alamosaurus* and *Tyrannosaurus* *rex* clomped around. The skitter of sand
lizard and blue whiptail under each base means someone put too much
sunscreen on but the sun is almost gone the stone is orange
the sky orange our boots dusted orange my brown
skin orange too. I tried to climb one leg of it as
high as I could. I asked permission from
the Ranger. He said it was fine but
the other side of the arch's leg
opened up to a cliff, a sheer
drop-off— the kind where
it would take days to retrieve my
broken body if I fell. So I stopped, clawed,
rested, nestled, and hugged the leg of the arch
and scooted inch by inch all the way down until
my husband caught me. I jumped into his arms my sons
looked on amazed or maybe something like embarrassed at their
mother who was not even eight feet off the ground but I swear
it felt like sixty when you aren't used to being surrounded by
gigantic portions of rock and red dirt and these rocks—lit red from
the sun—seemed poised to tumble if you breathed too hard.

Scattered rocks look like
giant cones of peach sherbet
just before they melt.

DARK CHOCOLATE UNIVERSE

Some people are perfectly fine without it.
Ross jokes that he can go for months at a time

and not even notice. I also felt like that about
dark chocolate—that is, until recently. Things

you can buy made of chocolate: a camera,
teapot, key, golf ball. A complete tool kit:

hammer, wrench, saw, pliers. Food shapes:
an orange, a piece of toast with egg and bacon

on top (complete with a chocolate fork and knife).
You can buy a box of Brussels sprout–shaped

chocolates painted green. Also green: chocolate
Yoda. Chocolate chess sets, a watch, handcuffs,

a gun with chocolate bullets, a high-heeled shoe,
a rose, bunnies, a pair of lips, and for someone

truly out of this world, you can buy a whole
chocolate solar system of planets (minus Pluto,

much to my chagrin). Someone somewhere
once imagined a whole solar system of chocolate,

maybe to soothe a loneliness bubbling up.
These days it feels like perhaps we could orbit

into an entire universe of chocolates, something
to help ease our losses, big and small. Maybe just

to gallop to a few stars, or to the Horsehead Nebula, for
all of the loved ones we've lost and still miss.

GIANT CLAM ZUIHITSU

Bolinao, Philippines

I remember the foot. I sank, fully submerged. I held the arm of the diver that chaperoned me to this giant clam farm.

When we were about three feet from the ocean floor, my guide shone a spotlight on the neat rows of beach ball–sized bivalves.

Cartoons and sci-fi made me believe they'd be much, much larger— large enough for a mermaid to take a nap, like her own secret underwater mini-fortress.

~~~

I'd seen the babies. I shook them in my hand like a pair of dice.

Or maybe a handful of molars.

The guide gently reminded me they were alive, not toys. I set them back in the small tanks, whispered *sorry, sorry* to each one.

Crisis rates of clam poaching in the area devastate the delicate coral reefs. These reefs depend on giant clams for their sperm and eggs—a major food for small fish, which in turn, are major food for larger fish, and so on.

These clams are the only ones that don't cling to stones or coral so people steal them from the ocean, even in so-called protected zones.
~~~

Groups of poachers swim out two or three at a time at sunset and hoist a giant clam from the bottom of the ocean, walking along the sea floor until they reach a "safe" zone, then heave the clam into their already waiting boats tethered nearby.

~~~

The only thing the giant clams have for protection is size—mature adults weigh over five hundred pounds. They sit four feet wide, nestled in the sandy floor. Most poached giant clams don't get a chance to grow. They are plucked while they are still "teenagers."

In this seeding zone, bordered off with netting and wooden stakes, I thought I'd see the mature valves of these larger clams blow open and shut, open and shut, open and shut, open and shut, open and shut— letting a clownfish tickle through their beards, just like in the cartoons.

Nothing prepared me for the way their wavy smiles clanged shut, as if to hold on to their day's gossip when I snorkeled near.

I placed one flipper carefully into the ocean floor, taking care not to break or even nudge a coral shoot. The clams lined up in strict rows so austere, like I had just interrupted a graveside funeral.

Except the clam closest to me was in a festive mood. Between all the colorful branches of coral at my watery horizon, I did not notice how he silently opened his hinged shell, letting his sloppy blue foot slurp and drag on the ocean floor, a small cloud in the otherwise clear water.
~~~

I screamed when it slid up onto the full length of my bare leg.

Giant clams want to help the ocean. These hermaphrodites release a
burst of both sperm and eggs multiple times a year, quite content
to broadcast spawn on the ocean floor. But too many humans want
their shells.

Too many want to fashion them into bathroom sinks. It's rare to find
a five hundred pounder anymore—a wise old adult—bearing witness
to generations of fish-story, reef-story, and various algae tribes.

Maybe someday when I return to the Philippines with my children,
we might be able to see the giant clams I planted, still parked.

And if more poachers get caught, we might we might we might—
see how clams can grow so meaty, so sneaky-silent in the dark.

BIG NIGHT

"Throughout the course of the generations, men constricted the night."
—JORGE LUIS BORGES

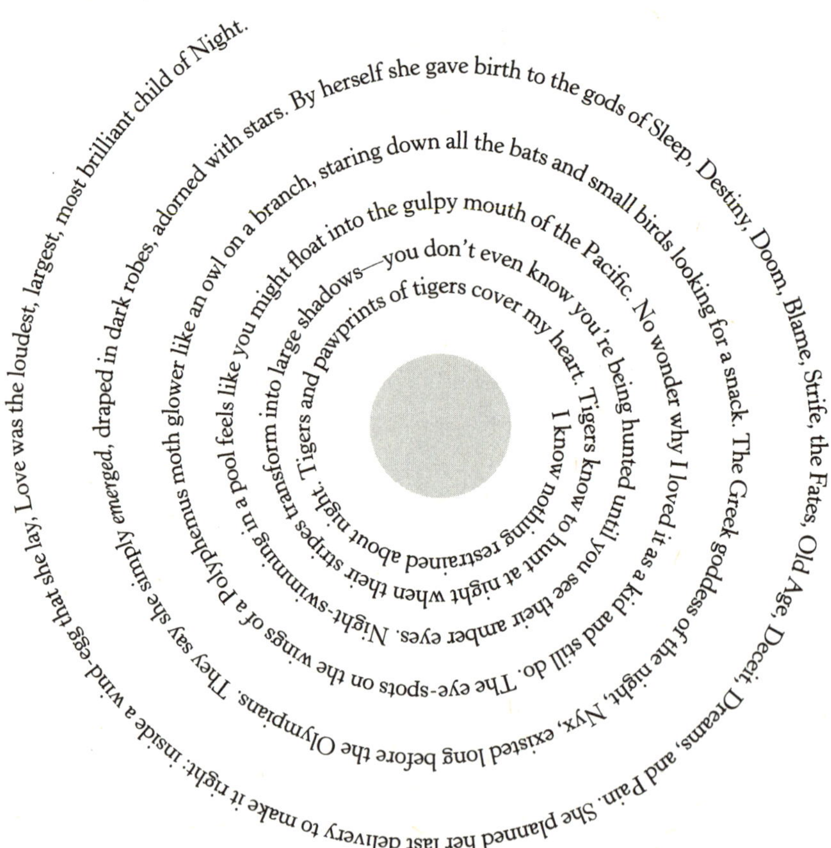

Tigers and pawprints of tigers cover my heart. I know nothing restrained about night. Tigers know to hunt at night when their stripes transform into large shadows—you don't even know you're being hunted until you see their amber eyes. Night-swimming in a pool feels like you might float into the gulpy mouth of the Pacific. No wonder why I loved it as a kid and still do. The eye-spots on the wings of a Polyphemus moth glower like an owl on a branch, staring down all the bats and small birds looking for a snack. The Greek goddess of the night, Nyx, existed long before the Olympians. They say she simply emerged, draped in dark robes, adorned with stars. By herself she gave birth to the gods of Sleep, Destiny, Doom, Blame, Strife, the Fates, Old Age, Deceit, Dreams, and Pain. She planned her last delivery to make it right: inside a wind-egg that she lay, Love was the loudest, largest, most brilliant child of Night.

AT MY BIRTHDAY PARTY
IN DEATH VALLEY
NATIONAL PARK

I told my friends: Please—no songs, no cake—just walk
with me here in the desert. But at night, sphinx moths clap
their wings and applaud under starlight when they shimmy
over brown-eyed primroses, shivering pollen all over the place.
Pleiades and planets twinkle-shook too as if to say *you get*
a party out here whether you want it or not. Thank goodness
my friends didn't listen, I mean my outside pals—the salt flats,
ancient waters, the chthonic ghosts of tiny pupfish found nowhere
else in the world, wriggling out of the creek beds with eyes the size
of this lowercase o. Thank you, super blooms of purple mat flowers,
the dazzle of people gathered who've loved me for over twenty years,
for us all looking at the thousands of stars and Orion's Belt
on this ghostly winter night—thank you for still being able
to gasp at the waxing moon, giving us all such a very good glow.

HUMMINGBIRD ABECEDARIAN

Arriving with throats like nipped roses, like a tiny
bloom fastened to each neck, nothing else
cuts the air quite like this thrum to make the small
dog at my feet whine and yelp. So we wait—no
excitement pinned to the sky so needled, our days opened
full of rain for weeks. Nothing yet from the ground speaks
green except weeds. But soon you see a familiar shadow
hovering where the glass feeders you jangled and brought
inside used to hang because the ice might shatter the pollen
junk and leaf bits collected after this windiest, wildest of winters.
Kin across the ocean surely felt this little jump of blood, this
little heartbeat, perhaps brushed across my grandmother's
mostly gray braid snaked down her brown
neck and back across the Indian and the widest part of the Pacific
Ocean, across the Mississippi, and back, slinking underneath my
patio. I've lost track of the times I've been silent in my lungs,
quiet as a salamander, those times I wanted to decipher the mutter
rolled off a stranger's full and beautiful lips, only knowing it was
spoken in Malayalam—my father's language—and how
terrific it'd sound if I could make my own slow mouth
ululate like that in sorrow or joy. I'm certain I'd be
voracious with each light and peppered syllable
winged back to me in the form of this faith, a gift like
xenia offered to me. And now I must give it back to this tiny bird, its
yield far greener and greater than I could ever repay—a light like
zirconia—hoping for something so simple and sweet to sip.

BLOODFLOWER

Sometimes my gentle father texts me warnings
or jokes, or water bird photos from his walk

around the lake in central Florida. Once, my father
texted me what to do if an elephant charges:

watch its ears. If they are pinned back, apparently
you have just seconds before it attacks. And last week

my father sent tips on how to survive a python bite:
throw mouthwash on its face or stab it with a saw.

Neither of which I carry on my person. I live
in Mississippi. I was more afraid of people

when I lived in Western New York. How they
used to smile and ask you to sign a guest book,

but stared and followed you while you browsed
the paintings. Started to approach if you stood

in front of one too long, the surveillance like being stabbed
with a pen on your way out of the gallery. I cannot figure

out how to make my tongue loll the way the locals
I love here say *oil* and I can't figure out the red burst

of a flower my gentle neighbor grows in a ceramic pot
on her porch, and she has long forgotten the name

so I look it up. The stain of it. The rain of it.
Its name sloshes inside of me. Inside of you too.

IN PRAISE OF
THE BUMBLE BEE ATLAS:
A ZUIHITSU

Are you flower visiting? Do you require nectar? Are you nectar seeking? The bumble bee sleep involves a sneaking of naps inside of a flower—some dusted with pollen sugar and I want that too before you tuck me into bed. Sign me up. The lemon cuckoo bumble bee sports a neat rectangle of gold hair on its bumble.

Color determines what kind of species. Also is the cheek length long or short? Is there a circle or stripe between the wings? Is there a black notch or V behind the wings? Is there hair in front of the face? On top of the head?

When bumble bees buzz near tomato flowers, the flowers release pollen because of the vibration. The result is a veritable disco party with thrown pollen lights like from a mirror ball dangling in the garden.

How does a queen become a queen? Who among the blue hyssop, prairie clover, beardtongue, tick trefoil, scarlet globemallow, vetch, and bergamot decides?

Endangered Bees:
    American Bumble Bee
    Crotch's Bumble Bee
    Franklin's Bumble Bee
    Morrison Bumble Bee
    Obscure Bumble Bee
    Rusty Patched Bumble Bee
    Southern Plains Bumble Bee
    Variable Cuckoo Bumble Bee
    Western Bumble Bee
    Yellow Banded Bumble Bee
    Yellow Bumble Bee

Can you draw from memory any one of these (above)? If not,
you better learn their faces, which ones show dots on their thoraxes,
how many abdominal tergites they have (so few actually have stripes,
despite what cartoons say). And how can we identify a bumble, if not
for the stripes, the stripes?

PILLOW TALK ARS POETICA

Is it possible to make a world where every head has a pillow?
Could we pillow the entire country, the entire planet? Maybe
organic cotton cases and eco-friendly fillings, of course. Those
who sleep alone (and don't want to) would have a pillow to hold,
and one to hold them at the same time. A man I once danced
with said his favorite word was *almohada*. When twilight ends
I am no longer sad, especially tonight when the harvest moon
lights each tree like the light hatched fresh from an owl egg.
When twilight ends, I walk through a cloud of perfume—my
throat colors the end of the day, little lantana creating such an
attitude in my mouth! What began was a glorious night not
meant for sleep. When we first danced, I wrote a paragraph of
leopard steps all over the tiled floor until I remembered I also
held a roar. And then—I wrote a book.

sunset

FIREFLY NOCTURNE

I never feared the dark. I welcomed it, let it rush
into my unbuttoned blouse. When I was a girl,
I learned the light of a firefly signals *summer*.
Signals *heart*. *Bare skin*. There is a certain sparkle
of beetles that knows how to blink in synchronicity—
a visual heartbeat in the darkest owl-filled atria
of a forest. Once, we held our own universe
in the morning rain. And like the firefly, I've mistaken
too many cars too many street and porch lights
for small moons. In late spring, the first branchlets
of bee balm and calendula color the air. Eventually
peeping frogs shiver awake when it turns warm again.
When we are old, I hope the firefly conversation we have
still thumps and thumps. I hope it's still green-gold.

WHEN YOU ARE NEAR,
I TURN INTO A BAJA FAIRY
DUSTER AT NIGHT

By which I mean I look like that flower that fireworks in midsentence
in the sky, over the end of a sweaty ball game. The crowd makes its way
to their cars while popcorn-spill & multicolored chocolate candies melt
into concrete steps. Maybe I mean you make me want to live
beachfront—so I can taste the salt & cliff-twist on each red stamen.
When you're near, you call hummingbirds to my throat & we throw
our heads back and stomp our feet from laughing too loud in a café.
I make good tears in my eyes, which means joy & maybe emerald
feathers fall to the floor. All the other patrons turn to glare: how
dare we delight in the swoop of blossom & neck. I know
it sounds like turning into a plant would not be fun, but have you *seen*
a Baja fairy duster? The way it shocks the mountain trail, how
it asterisks all year round? Perhaps you think I'd be sad to rely
on sunlight & sea spray, that I would wither in the dark, but trust me—
some people wait whole pink & proper lives to feel this even once.

BODIES IN THE AIR

If you want to talk tonight, just say the word, Hummingbird.
I want to know when you will flic-flack from crepe myrtle

or beautyberry bush. In Morocco's Erg Chebbi desert,
spiders cartwheel down sand dunes and how can you

not smile when you learn there's an Italian insect
called *graminicola* that somersaults in the forest?

Splash tetras leap from the river onto leaves fin-stuck
and marcescent, just long enough for eggs to grow

then swell into a very fine fry. Salamanders backflip
over the face of a rock to avoid owls, whip their tails

up and over, throw their long backs till their tiny forelegs
reach for the clouds. So when you finally speak it into the air

and let it leap off—remember it's the only moony thing
I've ever wanted from you. I want to see your words

hover in the air—watch them be the only feathered thing
on this blue planet that zips backwards, even upside down.

FIRST TIME BRUSHING
TEETH NEXT TO YOU

When I say *first time,* that surely implies
there will be a second, a fourth, a ninety-ninth.
From far away our teeth must look like Tic Tacs,
Chiclets, or moons of a faraway planet. Nocturnal
animals can smell better at night because scent
lingers when the air is still, and so I smell the mint
of our mouths but also the spill of peppers
from the salsa dropped on your shirt. The greasy
sidewalks we walked an hour earlier. Hotel soap freshly
bubbled and wet in the dish. When I root through
the thicket or the brush pile, my fur turns electric-striped
and tail-tumbled. I foam at the mouth. The mask
on my face means *bandit.* Turns out I love the dark.
My little paws want to grab everything and wash it.

POSTCARD FROM THE JARDIN DU PALAIS-ROYAL

What if these pink chestnut trees didn't offer shade or place to hide,
but let me finally face the sun again? And what if the Eden roses
(so creamy pink) didn't prick me when I leaned in close to drink
their sweetness, like trays of milkshakes ready to be served? So used
to spoilt fruit, berries past salvaging into a pie, when you came along
and wanted to make and bake with me. Wanted to poem with me.
My first trip without you and this is how I know it's real: I already
want to come home. In another life I always ran away, slammed phones,
apologized for everything. I'm in this garden nibbling a pastry and have
a new pen and notebook in a paper sack I shall bring home for you.
I want to always come home to you. The spring light here in Paris
turns everything lavender-edged, as if we stepped out of a bath, toweled
off in a gauzy twilight. What if we paused under a tree to chat with it?
What if what emerges green is our most tender shoot, most true love?

ODE TO SITTING
IN A BOOTH

It's the closest thing to a cave. I have
to resist this wild urge to carve a name
or word in it. My favorite way to sit here
is with cold vodka & grapefruit juice
& whatever bitter concoction you're sipping.
Under the table I'll nudge you with my heels—
a sign no stalactite or dripstone will stop us.
Bats do not require energy to claw-dangle
upside down. All they need is to relax
& gravity & there's plenty of both here.
No matter how loud this bar, within these three
vinyl walls we can drop electric into flight. We can
pretend we don't answer to anyone—not even
the waitress—& no one even knows where we are.

TO SEE THE VEINS

Before we were married, Dustin drove four hours from where he lived in Ohio to western New York to visit me. He smiled and laughed so much easier than any man I'd known, dug holes in my yard to plant wood lilies on his days off. I pointed, he dug. Any time digging in the garden was luxury. Any time in the garden for a woman he just started dating a few months ago was generous. Summer days when I had the windows open, I could hear my nosy neighbors gather on the sidewalk in

front of my house and worry over "The Hindoo" all alone, doing yardwork by herself. The space between my eyebrows scrunched up with my scowl: I'm *Methodist*. When our eldest was just two, he loved to tromp in between the blue lobelia and red columbine his dad planted years before in what became our first home. We called our son our garden gnome because he would dig with his toy trowel and pretend he was helping us plant crocus to naturalize all over our lawn in the spring. I remember little mounds of sod and dirt flung over his shoulder and into small piles like a tiny mole had started to ravage our lawn but got distracted. And he did get distracted: we all did. A baby brother joined him the next year and still they scurry and jump and run and climb and run into the woods whenever they get a chance. Here in Oxford, Mississippi, Dustin and I make and remake and revise our garden. In revision, we surprise ourselves with wins and losses. We

trace out the garden in the largest corner of our backyard. Our sons still check around the garden to see if any monarch caterpillars munch on the remnants of swamp butterfly weed. The last of the chartreuse chrysalises have cracked open along our fence line. But you never know what surprise flies up in a garden. Here in Mississippi no one asks where I am *really* from, like they do everywhere else. They just let me select red peppers and organic strawberry ice pops in peace at our farmers market every Tuesday. Here in Mississippi I still want to know the names of everything I plant: aster, wax mallow, and the difference between bee balm and bee blossom. Knowing names correctly is everything— it's a key to connection and tenderness and a turn to kindness. Maybe if you knew that swallowtail butterflies nibble pipevine, you wouldn't be so quick to mow the fields of it on the side of the highway. Or maybe if you knew that indigo buntings (which are bluer than a

Mississippi summer sky), and not just "some birds" hang around a place called *Sky Lake*, you wouldn't dump garbage in their home. Even the false dragonhead in our garden doesn't ask what I am. Neither does hyssop or Radio Red sage. If I don't know something, I look it up. I ask my gardener pals. I sketch it. Smell it. I carefully break off a leaf, hold it up to the light to see the veins inside. Like my veins. Like Dustin's. Like our sons'. And yours and yours too. It's the least I can do.

SOMETIMES I HAVE HELIOPHILIA

Desire to stay in the sun/love of sunlight

Don't call it an affliction—
call it *affection*. I'd stay under
the sun all day, never hiding
under a copse of trees if I knew

I wouldn't burn but isn't it
more accurate—that I burn
for the sun? To be pulled to the light
is nothing to be ashamed of: look

at flowers, butterflies, seals lounging
on a rock. Rhubarb sings in dark gardens
but truth be told it sounds more like
a wet cracking and popping. I think

it secretly counts the hours till it can turn
towards the sun again. For me the sun
has always been easy to love, as easy
as it is to love whatever small light

bees bestow on fallen leaves—easy
to love the light they give just before
they crawl into a honey-hungry sleep,
just before the first fall of snow.

GREEN LOVE POEM

Over the years, my feelings for you
are a *tweeblaarkanniedood*—a plant
that never dies. The leaves just grow
and sprout, some growing older

than catfish, older than cenotes.
When the first tender shoots
of lettuces unfurl, the green grows
fresh, electric in our garden, taste

that good crunch in the first bowl
of salad each year. If you don't eat
a nectarine outdoors while you squint
in the sun, and a few drops of juice

land on your shirt, can you really say
it's summer? What if indigo buntings
call out their little *thwips* and nobody
answers back to their syllables except

the squeak of tomatoes rubbing
together in the bucket of my skirt.
I celebrate you in sunshine,
I celebrate you on my tiptoes—

my whole neck stretched up
to receive your kiss. I unlock
you with a brass skeleton key
for a greenhouse filled with globes

of citrus. But there is your skin.
My bottom lip. My hands greedy
to learn how to rake it all up. How
to drink from a very full cup.

NIGHT AS A VERB

When I pull blankets up to the chins
of my little boys, I knight them.
My husband and I night for hours
and hours erasing bags from our eyes
or worry. Let me night like a flower
under the moon, moved to night
my petals—only when the sun nights.
Last week in India, a rat broke into
a dusty sidewalk ATM and ate over
a million paper rupees. It died after
that spitty wad of bills burst its
protruded furry belly. What did all
that currency give us anyway? They say
salt and ink lined the creases on his paws.
A seasoning becomes a kind of applause,
like smacking your hand on the table when
a meal is so delicious you want to shout,
you can't stop, won't put down the fork
or walk away until you night and night
and night before you finally say you're full.

WINTER WALKS: A ZUIHITSU

Yesterday I was followed by a mime wearing a xylophone harnessed to his neck.

When I stopped walking, he stopped playing.

I started to walk.
He started to play
I started to walk.
He started to play.
I started to walk.
He started to play—

This happened for two blocks. I turned a corner just to fake him out.
But he still followed.

I started to panic, because a. mime. was. following. me. But that panic is like ice inside your boot. Like a snake smelling your wrists when you bend to pick a toad lily from the mulch and muck of early spring.

Spurred on by soaring demand for seafood, a Spanish company plans to open the first commercial octopus farm next year but as scientists discover more about the enigmatic animals some warn it could be an ethical and environmental disaster.

A disaster.

At the company's research center in Galicia, northwest Spain, several octopuses silently propel themselves around a shallow indoor tank.

Once I lived and worked in a town full of pasty and soft people. Winter there was the worst. I could deal with people like that anytime, anywhere. But people like that in winter almost sank me. It took me years to say they almost did.

When I say soft, I mean it was as if they had no muscle, no heart.

My walks then involved waving goodbye to my snuggly, smiley starfish sons—still in pajamas—tapping at the window: *Bye-bye, Mama! Bye-bye!*

My walks then were through ice-scraped sidewalks with drifts up to my hips as I trudged to campus and any exposed skin turned blue like milk. *Bye-bye, Starfish! Be back soon!*

Further south, cacao leaves can move 90 degrees from horizontal to vertical to reach for sun and protect younger leaves from getting burnt.

Once, in western Florida, my horizon was the Gulf of Mexico and my father. Further down—my mother, to her left my husband, and beside him: my two children, all stooped over like a pack of dromedaries in the sand. Except this was no desert. They bent themselves for hours, searched for shark teeth, dark scintilla—shiny in the right light.

In winter, juniper berries mimic the sick-blue skies. Depressing to find you have remembered almost nothing of this season except this berry, collected by the wind—a puddle at your feet. I'm a summer gal, you reason. I bloom and bloom in the South.

What tragedy has happened when you find more than five doll heads washed up on a lake? Do children still hold a body in their hands while they walk? I have never put my starfish anywhere but first again. No job is worth it. Remember this lesson and you will avoid a tragedy.

Remember this lesson.

SOUTHERN NOCTURNE

Azaleas shout *me, me, me, me!*
when I walk past the statue
of the soldier who would've killed
or raped me if I walked past
someone like him in Mississippi,
1907, when he was first erected
in the middle of the square.
My friend reassures me: *Things
are different now.* The quiet soldier
looks me over as I scurry to my sporty
red car—the reddest car in town,
my student once joked. I am so easy
to spot along any street. I can lock the door
as soon as I get in and turn the ignition.
But tonight, when I drive home
in this heat, I wish I stopped first to slide
my hand against the cool marble, just
to touch his pant leg. See how it feels
under my brown hand, diamonded
by a white man, freshly manicured
by a white lady. I love this southern town,
the nights I come home to my sleeping
boys, a little dog who starts dancing
when she hears my car door slam.
Last summer, I was on an island
in Greece, surrounded by olives—wild

dumb luck since they beam a salty texture
I've disliked since I was a little girl.
Now most statues rumble and glitter
in museums. Sometimes I hear coyotes
scream fresh when they run alongside
the highway at night. I tell myself,
I can lock the door. I can lock the door.
In an olive grove, you can hate
the fruit and still love its light.

FOR ELEPHANT POACHERS: AN INVECTIVE

Bless the jasmine necklaced around my wrinkled neck.
Bless my eyelid half-shut.

Bless the bristle-brush hair on my tail my baby used to grab
when he strolled behind me. Bless my baby's grab.

Because you shot me with a poison stick and let me bleed
out, tracked me for days until I finally slumped in the river

sludge—you will forever see clouds as my ghost, rinsed
and risen from cinnamon shrub steam. You will hear

my whole family call a terrible call to you when you bathe
and you will look around and demand an answer from the red

underneath your moony fingernails. Because you skinned me
while I still breathed—because you wanted my skin

for medicine powder and blood beads to trade—my tusks
will shake in the space just behind your eyes when you sleep.

Because my baby will remember my smell twenty-six years later
and cry out with a bid so forlorn and pathetic, you will grow

twenty-six bristles of hair on the bottoms of your feet. Lovers
will shrink away. You will be too shamed to visit a public pool.

You will always sweat from your groin and wonder why all the wet.
The word *refreshment* will leave your vocabulary. Even the word *river*

will frighten you for the rest of your days like a dark venom
in your cracked gums. No one will want to touch your sweaty

center and strange feet and maybe you will remember the slice
of your saw against my face, my belly bloated and full of blackflies

when you came back to see if there was any more skin
you could trim. If there was any more juice from my eye.

TRIGGERFISH INVECTIVE

The last time I sank my face in the neritic ocean
I found only beige and bleached out bones, instead

of orange and green coral fans. I spoke to angry underwater
ghosts in other languages I forgot I knew—my mouth grew

full of seaweed syllables and cracked shells. Too many
pale bodies have marched snorkel fins over this coral,

snagged selfies on the coral, and scraped coral clean
of leafy food. Too many pale bodies don't even leave

a scintilla of small-shelled meats. The fish ghosts cackle
and hiss. Sometimes they answer with light-scatter.

The sea in this bay once curved full of cucumbers
and other funny vegetables, some with fin and some

with spine. Here the sea-swollen ring of motion bursts—
here the sea throws a dozen fish with pointed snouts

towards me. I never thought I'd be lucky to see triggerfish
in real life but they remain—almost a warning or last chance

for us. Why else would they activate their trigger fin
and hold on to coral bones if there was no more hope

of saving the bay? I am certain I will wear an anklet
of tiny bites from these 'humuhumunukunukuapua'a

and why not: for all the fish I see now, thousands more
swam just last year. And the last year. And the last.

The fish ghosts only send out mondegreens now.
Some scatter pale green light. Some scatter a cackle and a hiss—

WHY I HATE DEADLINES

In old-timey printers' terms it means nothing outside
the lines will be printed—but we all know what slips
outside the lines like color, like marginalia, is sometimes
the whole heart of what you really meant to write. And I really
hate deadlines—I mean every part of the word. I love curves,
not lines, and don't get me started on how I feel about death.
During the Civil War, Confederate guards drew a line around
the prison walls. If a prisoner crossed it—even accidentally—
they'd be shot. Let us miss every deadline. Let us draw no lines
in our lives, and if we do, let us color outrageously outside
them. Let the postcards I sent to you from even the Arctic Circle
make you understand I miss you because of my smeared
scribbles. Forgive me I was under a deadline
I wrote it so fast, I wrote it so smudged.

FLYING FRUIT

After a painting with the same name by Emlen Etting

Of all the citrus flavors in my amusement park mouth,
of course it's the lemon that leaps farthest. It makes my face

squinch and squint even when I know what's coming. Behind
that, the bite of an orange surges such a surf line, I half expect
to see a *Hawaii Five–0* wave crush just behind my tongue. After

that comes the lime, and it's not hard to remember our first kiss—
the zest and rest I finally felt with you. The rind is twisted

and torn into my glass of gin (and yours too) and soon we
are laughing too loud in the middle of the afternoon. Even if
we shuffle home, arm in arm, I promise to make moments

like these feel like flying. We're winners. We get to carry the goldfish
in a bowl home. We get to snack on funnel cakes and a sack full

of kettle corn. At home I'll serve us up a dish with a dollop
of lime pickle on the edge of our plates. Ring the bell. I will bring
the heat, the heart—you'll never want to get off this carousel.

TURNING FIFTY: NOTES ON A CENOTE

Puerto Morelos, Mexico

One day I'm packing lunches and the next I'm zip lining
across a cenote and letting go when I get to the middle,
deepest part of it. The twenty-five-foot drop into the crystal
water—a perfect cylinder of cool freshness set impossibly
deep into the earth. I shut my eyes quick in case I see one

of those cave tetra fish with no eyes: pale pink and mouth
drooped into a frown at all the bubbles and splash
I just made. Sara watches from shore. She bursts
into applause just like she's done for anything good since
we were fourteen. The water teal. My one-piece red. No clouds.

We rode bikes in the jungle. We passed notes in school before
cell phones (or any phone) you could hold entirely in your hand.
When we talked at night, we'd pull the long spiral cord
of the family phone from the walls of our kitchens, then under
our bedroom doors, giggling and whispering. Our parents

thought we were asleep. And now—we leap into cenotes,
leaving our sons behind in thirty-degree weather—
sons who have never known cars without seatbelts, a world
without padded helmets to protect their sweet heads.
In the last dark cenote—inside a cave—I cut my toe

on a sharp stalagmite. When I dove down to check what
I had kicked, I forgot to shut my eyes on the way back up.
At the edge of this cave wall, three tetras stared me down,
or rather, pointed their blank faces in my direction.
Our guide never mentioned if they were attracted to blood.

midnight

ROLLER-RINK NOCTURNE

When we try to pretend the moon moves
across our faces, we get a disco ball. Lightning

bolts and star-printed carpets glow fluorescent
yellow and purple under black lights. When

we get hungry and our hairlines wet with a song
of sweat, we pool crumpled bills from our pockets

and split a hot slice and a medium RC cola.
If you learn to skate backward, here, for a few hours,

you could be royalty. If someone asked you to skate
during Couples Skate, you were Empress Legionnaire.

If you could fold into a Romeo Slide, Cannonball,
or Shoot-the-Moon, you might as well be named

Supreme Leader Admiral of the Fleet. All you need
is practice. When we play at night, our eyes and bodies

don't ever forget. Our bodies remember the glide,
just like a river remembers each meander.

WHEN I WAS A VAMPIRE

In fourth grade, I wanted to be a man.
I mean, I wanted to be a vampire
for Halloween and I only knew them
as men—like Dracula with much might

and muscle in his neck. I liked the way
my friends looked at me when I first swore
out loud at school—the wild-pop of delight
and horror when I let loose with it.

My mother didn't live with us that year.
That and always swearing felt like blood
at the corners of my mouth. I checked out
theater books from the library to learn

how to shade a sunken cheek and studied
biographies of Bela Lugosi. My mother lived
nine hundred miles away that year. I waved
a shopping list full of items my determined

father couldn't find: spirit gum, liquid latex,
and fake blood—gelled like jam, I told him.
My mother was absent. I wanted to be a vampire.
I learned how to powder my brown self white

with poufs of baby powder all the way up
to my slicked hairline. Plastic fangs for a dollar.
I wore my own crisp, white oxford, a smear
of banana ketchup on the collar. I walked

into school straight as a licorice stick. My mother
missed the Halloween parade. When she saw
the pictures weeks later, she asked my father
how on earth could he do this, let me out

of the house like that? My friends won't believe
me now, but I was so close to being a man.
When I wore my fangs and clicked them open,
I felt a shiver of blood just under my gums.

WHAT DO YOU WANT TO BE WHEN YOU GROW UP?

(daytime)

Doctor
Attorney
Attorney for doctors
Chemist
Marine Biologist
Doctor
Attorney for scientists
Oceanographer
Geologist
Doctor
Ecologist
Meteorologist

.

.

.

If that doesn't work,
maybe
something medical?

Like maybe—

    medical illustration?

WHAT DO YOU WANT TO BE WHEN YOU GROW UP?

(nighttime)

A writer.

ADOLESCENT HAIBUN

Gowanda Psychiatric Center, 1986

I have to tell you sometimes I skated past the patients. The glint of barbed wire and spotlight only made me want to collect all the splits of light I could grab with my small hand. I have to tell you I was only twelve. I was an owl, or maybe a bowerbird drawn to metal, like the hot metal hoop on the court where the patients played pickup games behind barbed wire. I froze when my younger sister and I first skated past them. Pink plastic wheels, yellow pom-poms dangled from the necks of my white skates. I have to tell you, my parents told me not to go too far, don't be lulled by the pyrite and warm cream of their voices. Don't even think about going to the barbed fence—the electricity will pop you back further than the thinnest branch of oak above you. I have to tell you, I went there more than once: I wanted to see

the whites of their eyes,
their state-issued undershirts
damp. And not yet noon.

SOMETIMES I HAVE HELIOPHOBIA

fear of the sun

Sometimes we need a little glow in the wasp-quiet sky after school. Milky white light pink or beige or blue—the way our thin, brown bodies shine when the sun is out in full force. During sleepover games in the backyard, we cannot see each other. We are whole forests of ghosts. Sometimes I think people forget we glow some of us only show our full color at night like mushrooms like fireflies not tan not burnt but lit up with watery light from the moon and stars. If we are ghosts, we are ghosts *together* and that helps me breathe easy. The night always welcomes us, lip-glossed and perfumed for no one but us girls. The night is full of mice. The night is full of birds migrating above us, welcoming us budding musicians and artists and singers and writers who stay up too late without our parents knowing. Don't forget we are animals too we are animals we are not robots yet and we know so many animals thrive in the dark and sheet moss and still so many animals have full and frequent lives in the dirt. We can smell better in the dark when the air doesn't move. We are not dead. Our red and blue hearts glow inside us. We are not robots. We are here under the dense canopy of trees. We touch tree bark with wide open palms, we still laugh and hoot and shriek in the dark woods, we are here.

SUNBURN

What is the grief
of a sunburn? Who hurt

the sun that now hurts
you, wants to mark

your skin like a fresh slap?
When a Greek god places

a hand on you, what follows
is usually learning. Or terror.

WHAT IF MEDUSA

There are no published accounts of Medusa
ever turning another woman into stone.

    Not a single woman.

What if Medusa was someone who simply learned
to fight back against those who would harm her?

What if Medusa tried to steady her heart
when she found the sea god himself
suddenly behind her? What if she tried
to tell herself it will be all over soon if she just
kept quiet. If she let him do what he wanted
she could wash herself.
Try to forget it ever happened.

What if the only thing that kept her from crying
was a single bright memory:

her mother greeting her at the gate, a basket
of stone fruit still warm from the sun,
how of all her sisters—she let Medusa have first pick.
Her first taste of apricot, three bright syllables:
If I say it slow I can go back to that palace of light
with my family. If I say it bright and slow
and if I say it bright and if I say it slow he will
be done: *ah-pree-cott. ahhhh-preeeeee-cotttt.*

When the salt spray dries on your sandal—

when the figs and sugar-soaked walnuts dry

and crust around the edges of your dessert dish—

Who gets to call whom a monster?

SUMMER SONG (PLANTAINS)

No one wants a mouth
banana-colored but that
is exactly how she wanted
to wear this sweetness.
She thought the tiny fruits
looked like lipsticks. She
dared anyone to ask her
a question. She couldn't
wait to lick her lips.

GRAMMAR LESSON

What if sand is another form of the verb *to sin*?
As in—forgive all my sand, all this sand appears
whenever he is near. And when I'm not with him,
sometimes a veritable beach of white sand, pink sand,
black sand appears at the edges of the highway, hotel
lobbies, and sometimes even diner booths. But now
it's a beach—dotted with bright umbrellas and look—
someone left a pink-striped towel. You know
how it is—you are a good girl. You wore sunscreen even
on cloudy days in Sand City. And no matter how you shake
and brush it off—what never fails to stick is sand. Look:
I found a whole sin dollar. I found a fiddler crab with one
good claw. She waves and waves it—shielding herself
from the white heat and all the pop and crackle of this sin.

SPACE JELLYFISH: A PARABLE

2478 moon jellies were launched into space

and soon bloomed to over 60,000 jellyfish.

When it happens in the sky over Florida, everyone who looks up panics.

Getting more for free is good, right?

When the jellyfish returned to the ocean, they didn't know which way was up anymore

so they didn't know when to stretch to the light and when to stretch to the dark.

But getting more and more on this planet is so good, right?

Math time: if a rocket ship costs $62 million every time it is launched,

subtract the animals that die when debris plummets into the ocean at such a high speed

any bird it hits becomes a plosive, bloody mist. Multiply that

by being able to say you went to space to anyone who will listen for the rest of your life

and add to it because getting more and more and more

on this planet feels so good, right?

And if tens of thousands of jellyfish don't know

which way is up anymore, isn't that just fine?

PLUTO HAIBUN

after the light installation Pluto, *by Guy M. Hughes,*
Southern Illinois University

Beneath this dome of blue light on campus, everyone sleeps.
Marketing major with three kids. Teaching assistant who stayed up
all night scribbling on student essays. Random janitor. This glow
makes us all look like we sleep inside a fig. And maybe we do—our
mouths so full and spilling dark seeds and secrets. Soon there will not
be snow, only the ghost of snow. Like the spirit who once whispered
to me, *a yak's milk is pink.* I learned that just seven days ago and
shared it with anyone who'd listen. Now no one will talk to me. Our
skin is plum—plum for the picking while we doze and dream of the
galaxy and that farthest ball of ice that was demoted to a star. *O lord*
of the dead, take pity on us. We are not yet finished with this life.
We still have many books to thumb through, too many fruits yet to
peel and taste. When you stroke your purple beard at the sight of us
sleeping in a circle, please pass me by. Do not grab me by the waist.

    There will be plenty
    of time for me to bathe you,
    comb gems from your hair.

SUMMER SONG (THUNDER)

Why would you trust anything
that disturbed your little dog's
loyal heart? Why would you
trust a sound that comes before
a bomb-blasted wall or roof,
or a door slammed after a fight?
How in this world do you trust
a sound that visits before it
unlocks or opens a fresh wound?

COMPLAINTS ABOUT THE SILVER CREEK FESTIVAL OF GRAPES

(found poem)

I have always enjoyed the Festival of Grapes
                             except for last year.
Where is the parade?   Where is Elvis?   I was so disappointed.

Bring those things back!
    A beer tent is not a family day and it was always a family day.

There is nothing left in this entire town for my children.
    What about clowns

You do the Festival of Grapes
just for adults to get drunk in the park who you kidding

    What about clowns

You took the festival out of the Festival of Grapes.

What about face painting for the kids?
    What about clowns

I don't care about games. I never win anyway. My kids don't need
    another goldfish that dies before we get home.

My oldest made history by being the youngest grape stomper in the
world and now no more stomping no more clowns I fear the crafts
will be the next to go.

        I think honestly this is just a way to kill the whole festival.

How do you have a grape festival and no stomping?

    Just forget it—
        I'll drive over to the Strawberry Festival instead.

SUMMER SONG (URCHINS)

I can't remember if they see
with eyes or a nose, or if every
spike on their body pinpoints
a combination of both?
We've always been warned
to avoid them for the sting
the pinch and hot bite—
and because I was a very good
girl in ocean or land, I did.

SCORPION

I once held a scorpion in my bare hand.
My name in your mouth is *arachnid*.
My heart is pepper sick,
dark but holds fast.
A place for kindness rests
in my pocket, a possum
patch of ways to call me
anything but my name.
I don't even answer to it
when you stand in the same
room. I remember the scorpion
crawled to the table edge
of my open palm. The tail
held its very good curl—but
never once dipped into me.
Sometimes I have nothing
to write if I can't picture you
reading it. That stings a little.
But not when I've held
a scorpion in my hand—
I only felt a small tickle.
I want her to always read
my books and wonder where
your leg or lip turns up. Listen: if
I'm not afraid of pain in my own
soft palm—why would I ever care
what she might think of me?

AMERICAN TENDERNESS

I was born a snapdragon—from a burst of seeds knocked clean by a rabbit escaping a fox. When our skull-shaped seed pods are crispy and ready to shake, they spit seed. And when the fox had his catch by the neck—I could do nothing but grow, tipped to light in a bit of blood rain.

America, I am your good, brown friend. For many of you—I am the *only* brown friend you have. How I love being your good, brown friend. Very good. Very brown. Many of you tell me you don't see color, as if we're colorless, transparent, or rather—as if we're clear like Zima, Crystal Pepsi, hair gel, a varnish, seltzer, a gloss. I know many of you don't interact with many brown people (why is that?) and I'm one of your only sources of actual, lived experience as a brown woman (again, *why is that?*) but I'm here to say any violence or harassment towards me and my family was never, ever served to me by someone with brown skin.

Senior year in college:

I had to go to court to get a restraining order because a white coworker broke into my dorm room several times. The last time, I was sleeping when he broke in. I didn't have my glasses on so you can imagine my terror. I screamed and screamed for my life. O, how I can scream when I need to save myself. O how I can scream.

First year, grad school in Florida:
The two men who attacked me while I was walking on campus in the middle of the humid morning in Tallahassee during my first year in grad school were white.

In the middle of the morning.

I was mailing a letter to my parents telling them I was okay, I survived orientation. This was before cell phones. It happened on the way back to my apartment, after the envelope safely nestled in the blue mailbox with so many other letters to parents telling them their children were okay too.

I sometimes wonder what happened to that letter. Did it fly away? My parents never told me they received it.

I dropped out the next week and became a waitress in a mall and O—all the cash I made because I let white men in suits call me *Honey,* call me *Baby,* call me *Sugar.* So much cash. So much honey. But I took it and took it and took it all—I thought I'd never apply again to grad school but at least I had fistfuls of cash.

I thought my life in words was over. I thought my life in words was over. I thought my life in words was over. I thought my life in words was over.

When I go through the Rolodex of Awful Incidents in my mind—I have to tell you, all, I mean *all*—the times I've been followed or stalked or teased or bullied—have been by white men. So forgive me if I laugh at your fear and hatred of brown immigrants, or when you say immigrants are a danger to the fabric of our country.

Dear America, I am red clover. Every prick at the edge of the highway makes me consider my own red highway, mapping out very good blood to me here in Mississippi. What a riot of joy to say in spite of where I was scattered, today I am gathered. I was once scattered and now I am gathered. I am here, and growing dark waxy leaves.

Dear America, I am a magnolia now. Not the white bloom. The sturdy trunk. But I want to start with the milk. The cream of late spring, so many saucers spilling in the shadow of the milk moon, the flower moon— the moon of the fragrant month my oldest child was born.

For once, America— here in Mississippi, I don't look over my shoulder. It is possible even in this place. For once, America—I want to pour something like tenderness back into your cupped hands and your hands and your hands. And your hands, too.

the darkest hour
is just before dawn

PRAYER WHILE WAITING
AT MY AIRPORT GATE

Please don't let me sit next to anyone
who decides to trim their toenails,

    or someone who chews and sprays
    food with their mouth open. Please don't

let them spread their legs under the seat
in front of me, lay their head on me to nap,

    or tell me about this one Filipina or South Asian
    they used to know and ask if I'm related. Please

let me make all connections, but if I don't,
please let no one offer to buy me a drink

    then ask me to join them in a hotel room.
    And most of all, please let no one spread

their blanket over me too and whisper, *A little
slumber party for us!* into my ear. Just help me

    get back home to the city where all the lights
    scattered look like a sanctuary of lichen

glowing in the dark. Bless me with no one
in the seat beside me, round ice in my ginger ale,

    and a good paperback. Help me arrive just
    in time to always tuck in my owlets, and let them

want me to sit at the edge of their beds for a few
years more with my hand on their hearts, Amen.

FOOL'S GOLD

Joy because all the rocks could fit
in a little girl's fist. I was a girl who
wanted a little shiny treat on road trips.
Still am. My parents always dished out

rules at every rock shop while we stopped
to get gas in the desert: *Decide quickly!*
Just one! How to choose between
chalcopyrite, rose quartz, fool's gold,

a geode slice, or amethyst? That word
so pretty on my tongue and teeth. I liked
to tumble that word around in my mouth
while riding my bike or waiting

for the school bus. It made me think—
perhaps for the first time ever—of being
a mother. Silly now to think of it, but
I thought if I had a little girl, I'd name her

Amethyst. Amethyst—how I loved making
the *thyssst* sound like a snake! Out of all those
dusty bins in all those souvenir stores, I kept
selecting fool's gold, kept buying it with

my allowance for the best payoff, the best trick.
Sometimes I'd convince the neighborhood kids
to believe I had a pirate map. There was treasure
found there, in the suburbs of Phoenix. The day

before, I'd bury it in the labyrinth of ditches
in the cul-de-sacs of our little stucco homes.
We rode bikes everywhere. When we were
outside, our parents never knew where

we were. I'd lead the younger kids to the very spot
I chose before. We kicked and clawed at the dirt
until that familiar gleam shone. I didn't mean
to fill our days. I know they went home and told

their parents we struck gold. And we did.
The unbelievable part is *not* that the kids believed
me every single time. The unbelievable part
is I thought we'd have a gazillion more days like

this—sun-drenched and dust-decorated,
our hours stretched like pastel taffy. I thought
we'd have so many days, more days flying—
riding bikes until sunset, popping wheelies

when the coast was clear. I thought
our parents would always be at the front door,
flicking on and off the porch light,
calling all of us home, all of us fools.

THE IMMIGRANT'S VERY GOOD DAUGHTER

I know my mother loves me. She dressed me like a doll—
glossy black hair side-parted and clipped with a barrette.

She slid my sausage legs into white tights with pink
ruffles on the seat. Red Mary Jane shoes. I was a walking

Valentine to this country that she loves, which didn't
always love her back. I have made my mother happy.

She took me to so many doctor parties before I was ten.
There, I danced on command in front of her Filipino

friends, who clapped for me—their fingers still greasy
from trays and trays of party lumpia. I know

my mother still loves me. I bought a car, a house,
a lawn mower—all without a man. All before

I was thirty. Okay, maybe she was a little worried
that only a little dog would sit in that house

with me—but if she was, she never showed it.
I know my mother loves me: yesterday I showed

her my recent retirement statement and she smiled
and said, "Good, good," and told me I should still

try out for *Wheel of Fortune.* I know my mother
loves me: I have stayed out of the sun. I wear

wide-brimmed hats. Even so, my face is full
of freckles and she tells me I could have been

Miss India. Miss Philippines. Miss Universe. If
I was just a *little* taller. Just a little. My sons

are slathered with sunblock. My husband reveres
me. He eats everything I cook and smiles. But

I have not rolled a single lumpia correctly. When
I fry them, they burst at the seams, the meat

and carrots spilling into the pool of hot oil.
But I know my mother loves me. When I leave

her, she sends me home with frozen lumpia, made
well in advance of my visit, sealed twice in Ziploc,

and tucked in a small cooler. Each end
of the lumpia folded tight and neat, like

her secrets and wishes and hopes
for her daughter to finally, *finally* get called on

by a game-show host. One with a jaunty name
like Pat or Alex. She'll see me guess a consonant

or buy a vowel. She'll see me remember
to answer in the form of a question.

ONE VOTE

After reading a letter from his mother, Harry T. Burn cast the deciding vote to ratify the 19th amendment of the U.S. Constitution.

My parents are from countries where
mangoes grow wild and bold and eagles
cry the sky in arcs and dips. America
loved this bird too and drew it on dollars

clutching olives and arrows. Some think
if an eaglet falls, the mother will swoop
down to catch it. It won't. The eagle must fly
on its own accord by first testing the air slide

over each pinfeather. Even in a letter of wind,
a mother holds so much power. After the pipping
of the egg, after the branching—an eagle is on
its own. Must make the choice on its own

no matter what it's been taught. Some forget
that pound for pound, eagle feathers are stronger
than an airplane wing. And even one letter, one
vote can make the difference for every bright thing.

NURSERY

In high school, boys hardly ever noticed me, and when they finally did
years later, I could not imagine making a life with them. One called me
the N-word when I was seven. I needed a restraining order for another.
I almost got used to riffraff. So it still seems a surprise I ever had
the occasion to set up a nursery of my own. When I found out a boy
kicked inside me—a bright panic perfumed me and to be honest, never
left. I know almost nothing of boys but their father proved to me
a boy can grow to be a gentle man. If you look around, there is plenty
of *gentle* to celebrate: a male Darwin's frog keeps a nursery in his own
mouth, the leap of tadpoles is a reverse gobble-drool and what trust—
he won't even fever for a bite (and he never does!) as they jump
to pondlife and many breakfasts of chewy wings. The male seahorse
carries the dark swell himself in his brood pouch until he throws
a parade ending with a confetti of gallops. Scientists still don't know
where whale sharks give birth. I wish I could freeze the morning
I came down the stairs and found my two boys still in matching
pajamas, quietly drawing sea creatures. I wish we'd keep some secrets
underwater. Let us never find a nursery of those gentle giants. Let
them swim and grow into school bus-sized sharks, without ever
gliding into nets or boats. I wish for unsolved equations and maps
of the ocean always unfinished. I wish it full of unspooled, unfurled
tentacles solving for x where y means silver-bubbled plankton,
and c means a whole cadre of shrimp scuttling for cover—
an orange scarf vanishing into the coral when you swim too close.

SATURNINE

for P

When you told me you wanted to live on Saturn,
my hands grew cold like all the blood rushed
to my heart to help it in its purple panic. I never

even thought of losing you until then. Silly, stupid
mother—arrogant from each moment you reached
for my hand, reached for my neck, lifted your belly

to mine, or begged me for a snack. My darling—
every season on Saturn lasts seven years. When you
announced your plan of living among all those

jumping yellow moons, we would have still been
in your first long summer—seven *years* of that
heat wave with ice pops staining your mouth.

Seven years of collecting flowers in a butterfly net
for my pillow. Seven years of lifting the windows
each morning, a small hallelujah to hear the cardinal

spin a song over your bed. When you told me not
to worry, you'd visit, you'd come back to me—
all I could think of was the black-sick of you tunneling

through space without me. How blue nebulas might
dampen your very good cheeks. I know it will come.
That day will come. But today, let's enjoy the long summer.

Enjoy the mosquito bites, the little sandals chaos-flung
on the patio. Let's see who can make the biggest, most brilliant
spray of light when we bite into our cobs of corn.

ALMOST MERCURY

for J

In the throes of nine months' delirium,
we almost named our last child Mercury.
I don't know how else to say it—I sensed
him so clearly that last June inside me,
every vein & capillary felt rinsed clean
with this truth. I *knew* he was coming,
our littlest, our last. All six pounds of him—
a tiny nocturnal Roman god of fleet feet, more
clever than a coyote, chatty like a dolphin
with his clicks & kicks in my belly. Owl eyes
like mine. Trickster. The planet itself spins
with no moons, no rings, wrenched full
of lobate scarps across the surface like
giant wrinkles, nothing I'd want as a blessing
for our baby. Except this: time moves
so slowly there—holding him just one day
on Mercury would be two whole months
on Earth. That first day with our final baby
it might as well have been—it felt like I held
the rest of an entire, glorious summer:
sunflower & stone fruit & mulberries & bees.

THIS IS NOT A SAD SIGHT

It's the sound of your two sons praying over
a wobbly fish they named *Hephaestus,* half-floating
on its side in a forty-gallon tank. Your boys do not
know you look up from your book and watch
their two moon-faces worry-glow green through
the other side of the tank. They pray to one god,
not the Olympians, though if this fish doesn't heal
soon, they might start. Neither of them knows
how to pronounce *Hephaestus.* They just liked
learning he worked inside a volcano. These days,
I have to remind them to tiptoe and dust
the outside of the tank, have to tell them no more
fights over whose turn to feed their fish. Sometimes
even I forget to do it. These days, they have
baseball, tennis, piano. They'd rather get
dropped off at the ice cream parlor, get cones
swirled high as Olympus, and after school, wander
downtown with pals for an odyssey. But while
drafting this very poem, I'm crushed to edit—
as of yesterday: RIP Hephaestus, aka *Hay-FOO-STAY.*
As in, *Please let Hay-FOO-STAY wake up and swim
again.* The shield I now carry is different
from the one he made for Achilles, carved full
of vineyards and war—too much dumb drink
and battle—doomed weddings and dancing.

I've made my own shield, hammered
into a fine filigree, edged with magnolia leaves,
inlaid with pearl and gold. It tells the story
of two boys praying in matching pajamas—who
at one time actually *insisted* on matching
pajamas—who once loved their goldfish
named for the Greek god of fire,
the craftsman, the metalworker they admired
so much. The very remembrance fills their mother's
heart with so much magma, it might erupt.

PERIODIC

<table>
<tr>
<td>

My son has five or six shirts that feature the Periodic Table. The one that guarantees a flip for my dark mood sports a bold print of that famous chart and underneath in block letters: I WEAR THIS SHIRT PERIODICALLY. I can't help it—

</td>
<td>

I'm an easy audience. He loves the order, the minerals and elements packed in stacks and stacks of squares. The meanest thing he's ever done is tell his younger brother, Jasper, that J is the only letter missing from the Table.

</td>
<td>

Of course, J would burst into tears. But now my littlest guy learned a retort: *Jasper* means *beautiful mineral*—ancient Egyptians forged and set special rings of it for their Pharaohs and Queens.

</td>
</tr>
<tr>
<td>

Last week, my husband told us our bodies have enough graphite to make 9,000 pencils each. We oohed and aahed— and meant it. Yes, we are a family of nerds.

</td>
<td>

Periodically we fight, but never for long, and any wounds heal quickly. We've taught these boys how to apologize, how to look people in the eye when they say sorry.

</td>
<td>

Periodically, a storm smacks us hard in our sleepy town, nestled in Mississippi's *velvet ditch*. When lightning strikes, it's 54,000 degrees Fahrenheit.

</td>
</tr>
<tr>
<td>

That's another fact I once heard from my boys. And maybe that is the closest to the actual blaze I hold in my heart for them. I know one day my eldest will grow out of those shirts. J will not even want them secondhand.

</td>
<td>

Periodically, I will make plenty of mistakes. Many elemental or unavoidable mistakes spill out. My sons are almost teenagers now. I don't know how much longer I will write about them.

</td>
<td>

On dark days, I'll remind myself what sweetness there was just from lifting a child's clean and dripping body from a tub. And the chemical reaction I got from a fluffy hooded towel, and two giant eyes looking *up, up, up* at me.

</td>
</tr>
</table>

FIRST LOCKDOWN, WITH TOUCANS

When my six-year-old son painted birds

    during art class   his principal ordered a full

       lockdown because   an armed man was spotted

skulking in the woods nearby.   When I got the news

    I could feel my heart throb   in my neck.

     If you pushed   even a single finger to my arm,

I'd surely burst.   I think of baby toucans

     who fall out of their nests. Sometimes

    a person scoops   them in the bucket

      of her shirt   and brings   these fallen birds—

their necks not even fully feathered—to a vet.

When toucans are babies,   their beaks glow

      only the palest yellow—   the famous rainbow

         has yet to bite,

            has yet to show—

ALBUQUERQUE

At the eye doctor, my favorite part
is when they ask me to stare into
the autorefractor box and focus
on a tiny hot-air balloon in the distance.
I've been doing this since I first started
wearing eyeglasses at ten years old,
pink ones, and every time—the few
seconds of panic in the dark as my eyes
adjust to find the balloon. Last week,
I overheard my youngest son practicing
for the spelling bee. *A-l-b-u-q-u* . . . When
I heard my son spell the word correctly,
it's not that I did a double take, stepped
on the brakes, gave myself whiplash,
stopped on a dime, or froze in my tracks—
more like a balloon festival in my heart.
All the sandhill cranes and pinyon jays
in New Mexico cocked their heads
in our direction. Or maybe it was more
of a blooming—a bursting forth of purple
locoweed, scarlet paintbrush, and three-nerve
daisies at my feet. Wasn't he just taking his
first steps across the kitchen floor, reaching
for me in his footie pajamas, a mini-Godzilla
stomping cars into the rug? I want you
to know: the balloon is always there,
hovering just above the highway.

The burners? Lit. The envelope of air?
Full. And just when you think there's
nothing else in your peripheral, you see it
clearly—a roadrunner—his tail,
his feathers—don't blink. He's gone!

WHEN MILK IS A MEMORY

When the milk first comes it is gold. When the milk first comes it feels like a tug. When the milk first sprays across the bed, you laugh, but your eyes widen. When the milk is too much and the baby bites, you want to cry and dig your hands into your husband's palm. When the milk spills out and soaks your shirt and the bed—you wake sour to the baby's cry. When the milk slows and it's time to wean and you put cold cabbage leaves in your bra, you cry. When the milk tries to flow and the baby still sniffs around your chest, you cry. When the milk goes back to the body, back to your chest and vitamins back into blood— you feel stronger than ever. The baby still gets fat and smiles and all the crying stops. When the milk is a memory

you see a glass full of it and think only: bottle. When milk is a memory and your chest softens, grows smaller—you can press against your love without pausing and the baby will coo next to you in his bassinet. When milk is a memory, every tongue and hot breath to slow near your neck just becomes a cloud of rain-precipitate and your hand an umbrella to cup all the hours of wishing for milk missing the milk teasing the milk fooling the milk and you've been friends and frenemies with milk and when the time comes, milk never says goodbye. And when milk gets to where he is going—he never even sends a thank-you note with his squinched lettering, so don't even bother to check your mailbox for his licked flap, his canceled stamp.

SUNSET, DESCENDING

The attendant says
to put up our trays
once again I return
home at night I'm a bird
a ruffled night owl
a silly goose honking
good night I could have
left the next morning
but I'm a bar magnet
my boys are metal
or I'm made of metal
and my boys are magnets
or I'm a magnet a tuning
fork anything a compass
points to Polaris winking
at me before I'm plunged
under the cloud
my window fogs
just enough now
the clouds look smoky
like I'm on fire or glittered
or singed for just
a few seconds maybe
the whole plane is engulfed
but then: grids and curves
of the city carve into view—

the ribbon of the mightiest,
muddy river unfurls now
just my heart is on fire
not the plane
and I don't melt or molt—
I'm home.
I'm landed.
I'm safe.

ANIMALS IN FALL

A major bird-collision event occurred in Chicago, Illinois,
last week, killing nearly 1,000 migrating birds,
the highest number on record . . . the birds died after
colliding into the McCormick Place Lakeside Center
during the height of their annual fall migration.
—AMERICAN BIRD CONSERVANCY, POSTED OCTOBER 10, 2023

News of yet another bird strike
from too many lights, too many panes
of glass. When we work at night
with lights on, we might as well be

a snake thieving another blue egg
into its ridiculous mouth. And still—
I love the night for the quiet. I love
the night for the sounds. I love to think

under the sound of birds migrating
above me and a line of faint pink
just beginning to ink above the trees.
For my children, the days of dress-up

for Halloween are gone. For years
I pinned felt tentacles, stitched feathers
to their hoodies, or made a light-up mask
from papier-mâché and cardboard. Today,

the boys drove off to school; one quiet,
one surly over who knows what slight.
So much of what I thought I'd remember
has fluttered away. Each poem is a soft scrap

we tuck and poke into our nests. But why
should all of this make me cry? As soon
as they were able, we taught them how
to swim, undulate, pulse, run, and fly.

MY SON REMINDS ME HE
WAS LISTENING ALL ALONG

WHAT THEY DIDN'T TELL ME ABOUT MOTHERHOOD

Sometimes when they were young, I felt like
I was underwater and couldn't make out sounds
or reason or rhyme, only coral clicks and distant
whale songs. A shiver of eel near my ankle. But
trust me: one day you'll surface. They start
walking, then running, and then they sit behind
a wheel. Then *you* sit behind a wheel, driving away
from their dorm. They grow smaller and smaller
until they're as big as a guppy, and soon *this*
bubbly sea is not at all where you want to swim,
even though it's what you always wanted for them:
that they'd grow strong fins—iridescent, fully unfurled
in the morning sun—and curious eyes, big-bright and shiny,
but the only waves you know now mean *goodbye*.

CORRESPONDENCE

They never forget to write—
the beauty of the sandpiper
is how fast its legs type
a love letter to the sea.

A nocturne is a poem of the night. These nocturnes and the act of writing to (and through) the night emerged from my thinking on the dark, on nighttime as a place of so much hustle and bustle in the animal kingdom (of which we are members, no matter how some try to keep us separate). For me, a slight dilemma occurs because night ideally means rest since I work during the day, but it's also when 80 percent of my writing gets done, as the house and my beloveds go to sleep. But this is nothing new—ancient Greek poets used the night as a time and place of transformation too. A little bit of magic.

The "summer songs" series is an homage to Lucille Clifton's "spring song" curated by Sophie Heron for *Joy and Hope and All That: A Tribute to Lucille Clifton*. Ms. Lucille was the only person (not related or married to me) I allowed to place her hands on my pregnant belly. Afterwards she gave me (and my son, now in college) a blessing for our futures and I think of it often.

"In Praise of the Bumble Bee Atlas: A Zuihitsu": Information about various bumble bees is from the Xerces Society, with gratitude.

This collection gathers up a number of my favorite poetic forms to teach and write:

Abecedarian: an acrostic poem that conventionally uses the letters of the alphabet at the start of each line going down the page so the first line begins with the letter *A*, the second line with the letter *B*, and so forth.

Ars Poetica: a poem whose subject is the actual writing (or not writing) of a poem.

Carmina figurata: a poem that employs a shape using the words themselves.

Epistle: a poem written as a letter.

Found poem: a poem that repurposes text gathered from an unexpected place, such as an online review, a menu description, unusually chatty directions, and so on.

Haibun: traditionally used for recording a location in a concentrated prose block, and ends with a "whisper" of sorts to the reader in the form of a haiku.

Invective: a poem of anger, usually full of curses and/or insults.

Ode: a poem that celebrates a person, place, or thing.

Tondo: (my own variation) in Renaissance art, a circular painting, carving, or mural. In my variation, a circular poem ("Punctuation") is a combination of a carmina figurata *and* a tondo poem.

Zuihitsu: a hybrid form—neither prose nor poetry—that compiles seemingly random observations and juxtapositions that capture a specific mood.

The poems "Punctuation," "Discovery in the Dark," and "My Son Reminds Me He Was Listening All Along" were all made with the program found on wordart.com.

ACKNOWLEDGMENTS

Praise and so much gratitude for the efforts and editorial generosity of the following publications, where these poems were first published, often in early forms:

Academy of American Poets' Poem-a-Day: "One Vote," "Ode to Sitting in a Booth," "First Time Brushing Teeth Next to You," "Hummingbird Abecedarian"

The Adroit Journal: "Nursery," "Animals in Fall," "Green Love Poem"

American Poetry Review: "Letter for Noctiluca," "Night as a Verb," "Saturnine," "Adolescent Haibun," "Almost Mercury," "At My Birthday Party in Death Valley National Park"

The Asian American Literary Review (Book of Curses): "For Elephant Poachers: An Invective"

Asian American Writers' Workshop's The Margins: "Winter Walks: A Zuihitsu"

Colorado Review: "Bloodflower"

The Common: "Nocturne for Dark Things," "What They Didn't Tell Me About Motherhood"

Cream City Review: "When I Was a Vampire"

Disorder as Order: An Anthology of Zuihitsu: "In Praise of the Bumble Bee Atlas: A Zuihitsu," "Giant Clam Zuihitsu"

Ecotone: "To See the Veins"

Green Mountains Review: "First Lockdown, with Toucans"

Indiana Review: "When Milk Is a Memory"

The Kenyon Review: "Bodies in the Air," "Triggerfish Invective"

The Nation: "How to Make a Moon Garden When the News Is All Horror"

National Gallery of Art, Washington, DC: "Flying Fruit"

The New Yorker: "Roller-Rink Nocturne"

Orion: "Chocolate," "What I Learned in Greenland"

Oxford American: "Pluto Haibun," "Albuquerque," "This Is Not a Sad Sight"

Poetry: "Punctuation," "Space Jellyfish: A Parable"

Phi Kappa Phi Forum: "Southern Nocturne"

Pleiades: "Periodic"

Ploughshares: "When You Are Near, I Turn into a Baja Fairy Duster at Night"

Poets & Writers: "Firefly Ars Poetica"

Prairie Schooner: "The Immigrant's Very Good Daughter"

Yale Review: "Grammar Lesson"

Invisible Strings: 113 Poets Respond to the Songs of Taylor Swift: "Postcard from the Garden du Palais Royal" (Ballantine, 2024)

You Are Here: Poetry in the Natural World: "Heliophilia" (Milkweed Editions, 2024)

A Literary Field Guide to Northern Appalachia: "Firefly Nocturne" (University of Georgia Press, 2024)

Special thanks from the rooftops: my parents—always first in my heart, ready to share fruit from the garden with me at a moment's notice, which means love and love so bountiful.

To Joseph O. Legaspi, Sarah Gambito—songs in my heart's chambers. Ross Gay: you are a nebula, a star nursery. Thank you for always asking for a poem or garden report.

Sharon Wong and Dave Stephenson, Mark Steinwachs and Jarred Wilson, JoAnn and the DeRosa family, Ben and Lisa Percy, Sara Sutherland, Erin Austen Abbott, Meridith Wulff, Ron Degenfelder, the Manganaro family, Becky Harding, Nina and Joy Parikh and families, Cristina Veresan and the Nueva School, Deb Whitman, Jon Pineda, Oliver de la Paz, Patrick Rosal, Christopher Bakken, Allison Wilkins Bakken, Kimiko Hahn, Cynthia R. Greenlee, Matt de la Peña, Jason Reynolds, Georgia Court, Roxane Gay, the David Citino family for their support and love after all these years, the Ohio State University Alumni Association, the Chautauqua Writers' Center, MacDowell, the good folks at Square Books, Mississippi Book Festival, 'Iolani School, the Blake School, Smith Reads and Boutelle-Day Poetry Center at Smith College, Rob Casper and the Library of Congress, Judy Braus and the North American Association for Environmental Education (NAAEE), Ranger Karen at Yosemite National Park, and the ranger teams at the Dark Sky Parks, including Arches, Bryce Canyon, Canyonlands, Capitol Reef, Death Valley, the Grand Tetons, Hot Springs, Saguaro, Yellowstone, and Zion National Parks for answering all my questions with so much patience and good humor.

Thanks to Anya and Miyako at Blue Flower Arts for getting me around the world and home again, the Academy of American Poets, Sumanth Prabhaker, Ian Cheney, Meridith DeSalazar and Wicked Delicate Films, Melissa Alter Smith and her #TeachLivingPoets movement, and my colleagues and students at the University of Mississippi.

The U.S. Artists Grants made the final push of this book possible, so grateful. Charlie Buckley—no one else paints stars like you. Thank you for sharing your beautiful nocturne with me.

I feel so glad and grateful to work with the whole Ecco team and especially Sarah Murphy, editor extraordinaire and queen of kindness. To my fierce and funny agent, Laura Blake Peterson—thank you for being a champion. Thank you to Sarah Jean Grimm and Michael Taeckens for being bioluminescent. Thank you especially to educators and readers for sharing my poems and walking in the dark with me.

Pascal & Jasper: when people ask what took so long to write this book, I say I was happily working on you two—the two best poems I'll ever have a hand in making. Being your mother is the most important work and honor of my lifetime.

Dustin: thank you for making a nest with me (no matter the time of day), for twenty years and counting. No one else I'd rather see fireflies with than you.